Table of Contents

INTRODUCTION

Most every Southerner we know has memories of blowing the billowing tufts of dandelion seedheads to make wishes and clear all the wispy seeds in one strong breath. The plants make for strong childhood memories, though many grown-up gardeners find them annoyances in the garden. What's the deal with these plants? Are they weeds or welcome visitors? Turns out, they're something different to everyone. However, they're not only invasive weeds. Dandelions are also rather useful.

The common dandelion (Taraxacum officinale) is among the most nutritious and useful of herbs, with a long history of culinary and medicinal use." In fact, dandelion leaves are high in nutrients, including potassium, iron, and vitamins A, C, B1, and B2.1 For culinary uses, the leaves can be boiled or eaten fresh; the roots can be dried or roasted to make a sort of coffee/tea hybrid; and the flowers can be fermented into dandelion wine or beer.

Dandelion is native to Europe but found throughout temperate regions in the Northern Hemisphere. The leaves, flowers, and root of the plant have traditionally been used in Mexican and other North American medicine. Today, dandelion is promoted as a "tonic," as a diuretic, and for a variety of conditions, including infections and digestive symptoms. As a food, dandelion is used as a salad green and in soups, wine, and teas.

The roasted root is used as a coffee substitute. The use of dandelion in the amounts commonly found in food is generally considered safe. Less is known about the safety of taking it in larger amounts. Some people are allergic to dandelion; allergic reactions may be more likely in people who are allergic to related plants such as ragweed, chrysanthemums, marigolds, and daisies. Little is known about whether it's safe to use dandelion in amounts greater than those in foods during pregnancy or while breastfeeding. Read on to learn more about this flower.

USES FOR DANDELIONS: WHAT TO DO WITH DANDELIONS

Dandelions are some of the most easily identifiable plants, always recognizable with their rosette of leaves and bright yellow flowers that often pop up in otherwise green lawns. Some people spend the entire growing season battling dandelions. These people obviously don't know what a treasure a dandelion (Taraxacum officinale) really is. Although often referred to as a weed, the fact is that there are dozens of uses for dandelions.

Dandelion medicinal uses came about centuries ago, as did their use as a food source. Keep reading to learn more about dandelion uses, and how they're much more than just a pesky weed.

Are Dandelions Good for Bees?

Bees love dandelions. Not only are dandelions edible and nutritious, but they play an important role in ecosystems as well. For one thing, dandelions are one of the first early spring bloomers that bees, butterflies, and other pollinators seek out for their protein-rich pollen and nectar. In fact, dandelions provide sustenance for over 100 species of insects.

Plus their seeds and leaves feed another 30 species from birds to chipmunks. In your lawn, they nourish ladybugs, which in turn eat aphids, and they aerate and add nutrients to the soil.

Are Dandelions Weeds?

Dandelions are actually not native to the United States. Native to Asia and Europe, dandelions were introduced into North America where they now grow in all 50 states, almost all Canadian provinces and into Mexico. In their native countries of origin, dandelions have a lengthy history and have been used by the ancient Egyptians, Greeks, Romans and in traditional Chinese medicine for over a thousand years.

The name dandelion is derived from the French "dent de lion" meaning "lion's tooth," a reference to serrated leaves. The genus name Taraxacum is from the Persian for "bitter herb." The species name officinale refers to it being a medicinal herb once listed in official European pharmacopeias.

Dandelion Benefits

Not only are dandelions nutritious, but they offer many health benefits as well.

- ✓ The powerful antioxidants in dandelion help neutralize free radicals, and protect against cell damage and oxidative stress. Polyphenols, another type of antioxidant, may reduce inflammation as well.
- ✓ Dandelions may be able to help manage diabetes. Compounds found in dandelion

may help decrease blood sugar levels and lead to improved insulin sensitivity. Dandelion may also aid in the reduction of cholesterol and triglyceride levels, both factors of heart disease.

- ✓ Dandelion contains potassium and acts as a diuretic, which is associated with treatment of high blood pressure. It may also promote liver health and even aid in weight loss.

- ✓ Dandelion leaves may have a slight laxative effect and may also improve digestion. Dandelion root may be used to treat issues associated with the liver, kidneys, and gallbladder.

- ✓ Dandelion root benefits are numerous, and they have been used for centuries to treat gastrointestinal ailments. Fiber-rich, dandelion has been shown to reduce constipation and support bowel regularity, which may mean it can be used to treat other digestive ailments such as hemorrhoids and diverticulitis.

Further testing in humans is needed, but there is evidence to suggest that dandelions may also boost immune health, have anticancer properties, support healthy bones, and even aid in the regeneration of healthy new skin cells. You should always check with your doctor before using an herbal or natural medicine, but generally, dandelions are considered safe to consume.

Can You Eat Dandelions?

All parts of the dandelion are edible from root to flower. The leaves are most commonly used as a food source, and like other dark leafy greens, are rich in vitamin B2 and vitamin A. A single cup of dandelion greens contains twice as much iron as spinach, and over 500% of the required daily intake of vitamin K, which has been shown to fight Alzheimer's.

This herb also contains vitamin B, E and folate, as well as high levels of beta-carotene, a powerful antioxidant. Tender young leaves can be added to salads, while older leaves tend to be quite bitter. If you do harvest older dandelion greens, they can be cooked down to reduce the bitter flavor. The leaves are best harvested early before the flowers have emerged.

This is when they are milder in flavor. There are plenty of dandelion flower uses. They can be dipped in a batter and fried much like other types of fritter. You can bake with the petals as well. Petals from dandelion flowers can be used as a garnish over meat or vegetable dishes, or to make tea. Remember to wash the blooms first and remove the green calyx prior to use. The dandelion's flowers can also be used to make wine and even dandelion honey.

Dandelion roots can be used to make dandelion tea. Harvest and wash the roots and then run them through a food processor. Dry the resulting processed roots in a low oven or dehydrator until completely dry. Then roast them in the oven until they turn brown, not black. Bring the dried roots and water to a boil in a pan and simmer for 20 minutes: 2 Tbsp root to 16 oz water (30 ml to 473 ml). Strain and drink.

Are Dandelions Safe to Eat?

While there are many potential health benefits of dandelion plants, most need further study. Always talk to your doctor before using dandelion to treat a medical issue. Some people suffer from allergic reactions when they come into contact with dandelions. This tends to be more common in people who are also allergic to related plants like ragweed, daisies, and marigolds. If you have reason to believe you are allergic to dandelions, avoid consuming them.

Also be sure to only harvest dandelions for medicinal or culinary use from areas free from chemical fertilizers, herbicides, or pesticides. Always wash the plant, store it in the refrigerator until ready for use.

DANDELION

Dandelion grows abundantly in many parks and gardens. This easily recognisable weed was once a cure-all of herbal medicine and is still popular in food and drink.

Scientific Name: Taraxacum officinale

Family: Asteraceae.

Botanical Description

Bright yellow composite flowers crown an erect stem (up to 1-30 cm) emerging from a rosette of large jagged, green leaves. Older plants have a long tapering white root and younger plants have thinner roots and rhizomes.

Status

Perennial. Distributed in temperate zones.

Habitat and Distribution

Native to many temperate parts of the world, they are found growing in gardens, parks, lawns, roadsides, waysides, meadows, fields, orchards and woodlands.

Parts Used for Food: Roots, leaves, buds and flowers.

Harvest Time: Early spring to late autumn.

Food Uses of Dandelion

Dandelion-and-burdock is a popular fizzy drink made in the north of England. The root has also traditionally been used to make a coffee substitute. The leaves of the plant are considered to be very nutritious and can be eaten as a salad or fresh vegetable. In Asian cooking, for example, the leaves are used like lettuce, boiled, made into soup or fried.

The flower buds can be added to omelettes and fritters, the flowers baked into cakes, and even the pollen sprinkled on food for decoration and colouring. Blossoms make a delicious country wine and beer is brewed from the whole plant before it flowers.

Nutritional Profile of Dandelion

The greens contain vitamins A, C, E, K, B6, beta carotene, folate, thiamine, riboflavin, calcium, iron, potassium and manganese.

Dandelion Recipes

- ✓ Dandelion and burdock wild soda
- ✓ Dandelion root coffee
- ✓ Braised dandelion greens with maple syrup
- ✓ A simple dandelion salad
- ✓ Dandelion flower vinegar
- ✓ Hairy bittercress, dandelion and papaya salad
- ✓ Eva's warm dandelion salad
- ✓ Roasted cherry tomatoes with dandelion dressing

Herbal Medicine Uses of Dandelion

The plant has been used as herbal medicine to treat wide-ranging conditions, including stomach and liver complaints, diabetes, heart problems, anaemia, respiratory ailments, consumption (tuberculosis), toothache, broken bones and sprains, sore eyes, cuts and nervousness.

Other Uses

The plant provides a rich source of nectar and pollen for bees and other pollinating insects from early spring to late autumn.

NOTE: As a member of the same plant family as ragwort and daisies, dandelion may cause allergies. However, there are few documented cases of the plant's toxicity in humans.

DANDELION - USES, SIDE EFFECTS, AND MORE

Dandelion (Taraxacum officinale) is an herb native to Europe. The leaf, flower, and root have been used for various infections, but with little evidence. Dandelion is found throughout mild climates of the northern hemisphere. It contains chemicals that might decrease swelling, increase urine production, and prevent crystals from forming in the urine that could lead to infections in the kidneys and urinary tract.

People use dandelion for conditions such as swollen tonsils, kidney infections, UTIs, and many others, but there is no good scientific evidence to support these uses.

Side Effects

When taken by mouth: Dandelion is likely safe for most people when consumed in the amounts commonly found in food. It is possibly safe when taken in larger amounts. Dandelion might cause allergic reactions, stomach discomfort, diarrhea, or heartburn in some people.

Special Precautions and Warnings

When taken by mouth: Dandelion is likely safe for most people when consumed in the amounts commonly found in food. It is possibly safe when taken in larger amounts. Dandelion might cause allergic reactions, stomach discomfort, diarrhea, or heartburn in some people.

Pregnancy and breast-feeding: There isn't enough reliable information to know if dandelion is safe to use when pregnant or breast-feeding. Stay on the safe side and avoid use.

Eczema: People with eczema seem to have a higher chance of having an allergic reaction to dandelion. If you have eczema, be sure to check with your healthcare provider before taking dandelion.

Bleeding disorders: Dandelion might slow blood clotting. In theory, taking dandelion might increase the risk for bruising and bleeding in people with bleeding disorders.

Ragweed allergy: People who are allergic to ragweed and related plants (daisies, chrysanthemums, marigolds) might also be allergic to dandelion. But conflicting data exists. If you have allergies, be sure to check with your healthcare provider before taking dandelion.

Surgery: Dandelion might slow blood clotting and lower blood sugar. It might cause extra bleeding and problems with low blood sugar during and after surgery. Stop using dandelion at least 2 weeks before a scheduled surgery.

Kidney failure: Oxalate is a chemical that can build up in the kidneys. Dandelion might reduce how much oxalate is released through urine. In theory, this might increase the risk for complications in people with kidney problems.

Moderate Interaction

Be cautious with this combination:

Antibiotics (Quinolone antibiotics) interacts with DANDELION

Dandelion might decrease how much antibiotic the body absorbs. Taking dandelion along with certain antibiotics might decrease the effectiveness of these antibiotics.

Medications changed by the liver (Cytochrome P450 1A2 (CYP1A2) substrates) interacts with DANDELION

Some medications are changed and broken down by the liver. Dandelion might change how quickly the liver breaks down these medications. This could change the effects and side effects of these medications.

Medications changed by the liver (Glucuronidated Drugs) interacts with DANDELION

Some medications are changed and broken down by the liver. Dandelion might change how quickly the liver breaks down these medications. This could change the effects and side effects of these medications.

Water pills (Potassium-sparing diuretics) interacts with DANDELION

Dandelion contains significant amounts of potassium. Some "water pills" can also increase potassium levels in the body. Taking some "water pills" along with dandelion might cause too much potassium to be in the body.

Lithium interacts with DANDELION

Dandelion might have an effect like a water pill or "diuretic." Taking dandelion might decrease how well the body gets rid of lithium. This could increase how much lithium is in the body and result in serious side effects. Talk with your healthcare provider before using this product if you are taking lithium.

Medications that slow blood clotting (Anticoagulant / Antiplatelet drugs) interacts with DANDELION

Dandelion root might slow blood clotting. Taking dandelion root along with medications that also slow blood clotting might increase the risk of bruising and bleeding.

Medications for diabetes (Antidiabetes drugs) interacts with DANDELION

Dandelion might lower blood sugar levels. Taking dandelion along with diabetes medications might cause blood sugar to drop too low. Monitor your blood sugar closely.

Dosing

There isn't enough reliable information to know what an appropriate dose of dandelion might be. Keep in mind that natural products are not always necessarily safe and dosages can be important. Be sure to follow relevant directions on product labels and consult a healthcare professional before using.

DANDELION ROOT BENEFITS FOR CANCER, CHOLESTEROL AND THE LIVER

Dandelions have a reputation as both a granter of wishes and a dreaded weed and lawn nuisance. However, did you know that dandelion root is loaded with nutrients and boasts a variety of benefits to your health — just like dandelion greens and dandelion tea? What is dandelion root good for? This plant is low in calories, yet high in fiber as well as antioxidants, vitamin K, vitamin A and vitamin C.

Research even suggests it can help reduce cancer growth, lower cholesterol levels and support liver function. In addition to being rich in many vitamins and minerals that promote a strong immune system, dandelion is also readily available, easy to add to your diet and bursting with a signature, peppery flavor.

Understanding of Dandelion

Dandelions, also known as Taraxacum officinale, are a type of flowering plant native to Europe, Asia and North America. As a member of the daisy family of plants, dandelions are related to dahlias, thistle, ragweed, lettuce, artichokes and sunflowers. Dandelions produce many small yellow flowers, called florets, which collectively form one flower head. Once it has finished flowering, the flower head dries out, the florets drop off and a seed head is formed.

The dandelion seeds are then naturally dispersed by the wind … or those looking to score a free wish.

Dandelion Nutrients:

Although dandelion is often overlooked as just a pesky weed, it can actually be a useful addition to both your kitchen and your medicine cabinet. Many parts of the dandelion plant are edible, including the roots, leaves, seeds and flowers. Both the root and greens are packed with health-promoting properties and can be used to make everything from dandelion tea to super-nutritious salads.

Not only is this plant high in vitamins and antioxidants — such as silymarin, silibinin, curcumin, berberine and resveratrol — it also contains potassium, magnesium, zinc, iron and choline.

Historical Uses:

Just like other roots, such as burdock and ashwagandha, dandelion root also has a rich history of use in traditional medicine. In fact, the origins of dandelion as a natural remedy can be traced all the way back to 659 B.C. in ancient China. It was also used in Arabic, Welsh and European medicine and was eaten raw or made into a juice or tonic.

Traditional uses of the dandelion ranged from promoting better digestion to healing the liver.

Some Native American tribes chewed on dandelion root to relieve pain, while others steamed the leaves and applied topically to ease sore throats. Why are dandelions sometimes called "pee the beds"? In some countries, including Scotland and France, these plants earned the nickname pee-the-beds, or pissenlit in French, due to their natural diuretic effects that can cause increased urination.

Dandelion Root Benefits

What does dandelion do to your body? Here's more about what research has shown us regarding dandelion root benefits:

1. May Help Kill Cancer Cells

A number of studies have found that dandelion root may be useful in the prevention and treatment of certain types of cancer, including liver cancer, leukemia, pancreatic cancer, breast cancer, esophageal cancer and prostate cancer. For instance, a 2011 study out of Canada treated skin cancer cells with dandelion extract and found that it started killing off cancer cells within just 48 hours of treatment.

Another study in Oncotarget showed that dandelion root extract was able to kill 95 percent of colon cancer cells within two days.

2. Can Help Reduce Cholesterol and High Blood Pressure

High cholesterol is one of the major contributors to coronary heart disease. Changing your diet is one of the easiest ways to prevent high cholesterol. Along with limiting your intake of processed foods, including more whole foods like fruits and vegetables can help lower cholesterol. Dandelion root has been shown to help reduce cholesterol levels. In one study, rabbits were fed a high-cholesterol diet and supplemented with dandelion root.

Dandelion led to a reduction in total cholesterol, triglycerides and bad LDL cholesterol, as well as an increase in beneficial HDL cholesterol. Studies also suggest that dandelion may help normalize blood sugar levels and lower high blood pressure.

3. Rich in Antioxidants

Studies show that dandelion root is especially high in antioxidants, such as beta-carotene, polyphenols, coumarins and hydroxycinnamic acid derivatives — which may account for its many potent health benefits since this allows it to fight free radicals. Free radicals are compounds that form in your body as a result of things like stress, pollution and a poor diet. Over time, the accumulation of free radicals can lead to cell damage and chronic disease.

Antioxidants can help neutralize these harmful compounds and have been shown to reduce the risk of conditions like heart disease and cancer. When applied topically, dandelion also seems to protect against skin damage caused by sun damage, aging and acne.

4. Supports Liver and Kidney Health

From filtering toxins to metabolizing drugs, the liver is essential to many aspects of health. Dandelion root benefits your liver, helping protect it from oxidative stress and keeping it working effectively. In fact, folk medicines originating from China, India and Russia have long recognized dandelion's effect as a liver tonic, mostly due to its anti-inflammatory effects and ability to fight oxidative stress.

One study done in Korea showed that dandelion extract prevented damage to the liver caused by alcohol toxicity in both liver cells and mice. These protective effects are likely due to the amount of antioxidants found in dandelion root, as well as its ability to prevent cell damage.

Is dandelion good for your kidneys? In most cases, yes.

This plant is known for having natural diuretic effects, meaning it increases the frequency of urination, which can help keep the kidneys healthy. According to Mount Sinai Medical Group, "Herbalists use dandelion root to detoxify the liver and gallbladder, and dandelion leaves to help kidney function." For centuries, Native Americans boiled dandelion in water and took it to treat kidney disease, as well as other digestive issues like heartburn and upset stomach.

5. Supports Immune System and Fights Bacteria

In addition to its many other health benefits, dandelion root also possesses antimicrobial and antiviral properties that can help stop the growth of disease-causing bacteria and pathogens. A study in Ireland published in Phytotherapy Research showed that dandelion root was especially effective against certain strains of bacteria that are responsible for staph infections and foodborne illness.

Although more research is needed, dandelion root may be a useful natural method for supporting the immune system in fighting off bacterial infections.

6. Strengthens Bones

Taraxacum officinale is a great source of vitamin K, an important nutrient that plays a key role in bone health. This essential vitamin increases levels of a specific protein needed to help build strong bones, which is exactly why lower intakes of vitamin K have been linked to an increased risk of fractures and reduced bone density. Dandelion also contains calcium, which forms the structure of the bones and teeth to help keep them strong.

7. Promotes Skin Health

Each serving of dandelion supplies a hearty dose of antioxidants, which can protect skin cells against damage to slow signs of aging and keep you looking (and feeling) your best. Not only that, but a 2015 in vitro study out of Canada also showed that applying extracts of dandelion (Taraxacum officinale) to skin cells helped protect against harmful ultraviolet damage.

Some research also shows that dandelion could possess powerful antimicrobial properties, which can help block bacterial growth to prevent skin infections.

8. High in Fiber

Dandelion roots are a great source of fiber and are especially rich in a type of soluble fiber known as inulin. Fiber has been associated with several health benefits, especially when it comes to regulating blood sugar levels. Because fiber moves through the body undigested, it helps slow the absorption of sugar in the bloodstream, which can help improve long-term blood sugar control.

In addition to maintaining steady blood sugar levels, fiber can also protect against a multitude of digestive issues, including constipation, stomach pains, hemorrhoids, gastroesophageal reflux disease (GERD) and stomach ulcers.

Dosage and Preparation (Uses/Recipes)

Products containing dandelion come in a variety of forms, including tinctures, liquid extract, teas, tablets and capsules. Dandelions are abundant throughout backyards and grocery stores alike. While it is safe to pick dandelions from your own yard and use them, you should be sure to avoid areas where weed killer or pesticides have been sprayed and remember to wash thoroughly.

Gather the roots by digging a bit deep into the soil and pulling out all of the stems that the flowers may be attached to. Wash the roots well to make sure all dirt is removed before using.

Recipes:

- ✓ The flowers of the dandelion plant can be used to make dandelion wine or dandelion jelly, while the greens can be added to soups, salads and pasta dishes.

- ✓ The roots of the plant can be used in a wide array of dandelion recipes as well, but many choose to brew dandelion root into a tasty tea or soothing coffee substitute.

- ✓ Dandelion root tea and coffee are both natural, caffeine-free beverages that can help start your day off on the right foot. Plus, the potential dandelion tea benefits are similar to the benefits of the root, which makes it an effortless way to get in your fix in the morning.

There are many different methods available for how to make dandelion root tea, but it generally involves pouring hot water over the root and letting it steep for five to 10 minutes before straining. To make dandelion coffee, simply roast the root first by baking for around 10–15 minutes at 350 degrees Fahrenheit.

Supplements and Dosage Recommendations:

Dandelion extract and pills are available at some pharmacies and health stores. If you decide to supplement with dandelion, make sure to look for a reputable brand with minimal added ingredients and fillers. Although there's no official recommended dosage for dandelion root capsules, most dried/powder supplements contain between 500–1,500 milligrams of dandelion root extract per serving.

If using fresh leaves to make tea, consume about four to 10 grams daily. If supplementing with dandelion tincture, have between 0.5 to one teaspoon (2–5 mL) three times per day. Always read dosage recommendations for the specific product you're using, since these vary from brand to brand depending on potency.

Is it safe to take dandelion root every day?

It depends how you're using it and your overall health. Many people can safely drink one to three cups of dandelion tea every day. For best results, start with a lower dose, and work your way up to assess your tolerance and prevent any potential side effects.

Drug Interactions

Dandelion is very high in vitamin K, which may impact blood clotting. If you take warfarin or another blood thinner, you need to maintain consistent vitamin K intake to prevent interfering with your medication. Because it acts as a diuretic, this plant can have an impact on kidney function. It may also interact with medications that are broken down by the liver.

To avoid interactions, try taking dandelion extract or drinking dandelion tea two or more hours after/before taking any drugs. Medications that may potentially interact with dandelion extract and other products include:

✓ Antacids
✓ Blood-thinning medications
✓ Diuretics
✓ Lithium
✓ Ciprofloxacin
✓ Medications to treat diabetes

If you have any underlying health conditions, such as liver disease, diabetes or kidney problems, it's best to talk to your doctor before starting supplementation or making any major changes to your diet. This is especially important if you take daily medications and are considering supplementing with dandelion root extract.

Risks and Side Effects

What are the side effects of taking dandelion root? Dandelion is "generally recognized as safe" as a food by the U.S. Food and Drug Administration. For most healthy adults, adding this powerful herb to your diet is typically safe and beneficial, however there are several side effects that need to be considered as well. For starters, dandelion may cause allergic reactions in some people when eaten or applied to the skin.

If you have a sensitivity to other plants in the same family of plants, such as ragweed, daisies or thistle, you may also have a sensitivity to dandelion. If you experience symptoms like swelling, itching or redness, you should discontinue use immediately, and talk to your health care provider. Is dandelion root ever bad for your kidneys? Dandelion acts as a diuretic, causing your body, especially your kidneys, to produce more urine, which is the same effect that diuretic drugs have.

If you also take prescription/herbal diuretics, this may negatively affect kidney function and put you at risk for developing an electrolyte imbalance, so always follow directions, and be cautious if you already have kidney issues.

THE HEALTH BENEFITS OF DANDELION

More than just a pesky weed, Dandelion is jam packed with nutrients and vitamins and provides a variety of potential health benefits. The dandelion plant is incredibly nutritious, an excellent source of vitamin A, B, C, D and K, and minerals iron, potassium, and zinc and has been eaten as food and a herb for centuries. For over a thousand years, the medicinal plant has traditionally been used in Chinese medicine to improve the digestive system and reduce inflammation.

Today, there are multiple potential health benefits of the dandelion plant and many reasons you should include it in your diet or supplement routine.

What parts of the Dandelion are used?

The entire dandelion plant can be eaten cooked or raw, but we get different benefits from each part:

Dandelion Root - The root extract holds a lot of nutritional value and herbalists have used it in traditional medicine to help with liver detox.

Dandelion Flowers - The flowers contain the antioxidant properties and may boost your immune system. Did you know you can fry the flowers in batter and make dandelion flower fritters?

Dandelion Leaves - The dandelion leaf can assist with digestion and support blood sugar levels. Like spinach, you can sauté dandelion leaves and add to any dish.

The Full Health Benefits of Dandelion

1. May support blood sugar regulation

Animal studies suggest the bioactive compounds aid the secretion of insulin which is a hormone to regulate the blood sugar levels. The research showed glucose was absorbed by the muscles at a higher rate to be used as energy. Overall the study showed dandelion may normalize blood sugar levels.

2. May reduce cholesterol levels

High triglyceride and cholesterol levels are key risk factors for heart disease. Animal studies showed dandelion leaf and root extract may reduce blood lipids, including triglyceride and cholesterol. However, more research is needed on the effects for humans.

3. May aid blood pressure

Dandelion has been used in traditional medicine as it seems to have a diuretic effect which works to help your kidneys release more sodium into the urine flow. Ridding the body of excess fluid can in-turn lower blood pressure. The dandelion plant also contains the mineral potassium which is known to relax blood vessels and consequently reduce blood pressure.

4. Potentially has an anti inflammatory effect

More research needs to be completed onto this effect but the animal studies suggest so far that the chemicals in dandelion may have anti inflammatory properties. Our immune system responds to injury with inflammation to protect our cells, but long lasting inflammation can cause further damage. The studies showed dandelion reduced inflammation and may then relieve pain.

5. May aid a healthy digestion

Dandelion research shows it may increase bile flow, which is necessary for the digestion process and fat absorption. It has also been used as a natural remedy for constipation, acting as a laxative to empty the bowels. It contains the prebiotic fibre which has been shown to reduce constipation and promote bowel regularity.

6. May assist in weight loss

Some studies show dandelion to improve carbohydrate metabolism and regulate fat absorption. We need a healthy carbohydrate metabolism to ensure our body uses it as energy rather than fat stores. The studies have all been completed using animals and more research is needed on humans.

7. May support liver health

Animal studies have shown dandelion plant to affect the liver in a few ways. One study concluded dandelion to reduce excess fat stored in the liver and protect against oxidative stress, which can cause liver injury. Another study suggested dandelion root may help prevent liver disease by improving liver function and promoting bile production.

8. May promote healthy bones

Dandelion leaves are a rich source of calcium and vitamin K that support healthy bones. Studies show they can have a significant increase to bone density and overall bone health.

9. Antioxidant properties may reduce cell damage

Antioxidants can fight against free radicals formed in the body, which are free molecules that could cause damage to cells if the free radical levels get too high. Dandelion is a great antioxidant which could regulate the free radical levels and reduce chances of them causing cell damage and chronic disease.

10. May boost the immune system

Some test tube studies suggest dandelion can help protect against harmful bacteria and significantly reduce the virus cells replicating. The more you are able to help your body protect against harmful bacteria, the greater your immune system will be.

How to take Dandelion

As covered at the beginning of this article, you can eat a full dandelion raw or cooked to get the health benefits. However, this may not be appealing to everyone so here are some different ways you can easily add dandelion into your daily diet.

Dandelion supplements

Dietary supplements are a great way of breaching the gap in nutrients you are unable to get from your food. Dandelion supplements comes in form of capsules, tablets or dried powder. Dandelion is often used within a supplement formula and mixed with complimentary vitamin and herbs such as milk thistle, which also has anti-inflammatory properties.

Dandelion Leaves

You can fry or sauté dandelion leaves, just like spinach or other leafy greens.

Dandelion Flowers

You can boil or fry a dandelion flower and even make fritters for a delicious dish.

Dandelion root extract

You can buy dandelion root extract to add into hot or cold drinks and still gain the health benefits of dandelion.

Dandelion Tea

Drinking dandelion tea is a great way to get the health benefits of dandelion. You can purchase dandelion tea from some supermarkets or make your own by roasting dandelion root. Dandelion root tea has been known as a natural alternative to coffee as it has a slight taste similarity.

Fresh Leaf Juice

You can make fresh leaf juice daily just like any other green smoothie, jam pack your blender with nutritious green dandelion goodness.

Can I eat dandelion from my garden?

Yes, you can pick and eat dandelion root and plant straight from your garden. However, never eat any plant that has been sprayed with fertiliser or weed killer chemicals. So, rather than trying to kill every pesky weed with chemicals, you could think about the nutritional value first.

Possible Side Effects of Dandelion

As with all herbs, vitamins and minerals, different side effects may affect different people:

- ✓ Allergic reactions
- ✓ Diarrhea

✓ Heartburn

✓ Dermatitis in those with sensitive skin.

Ten Things You Might Not Know About Dandelions

Whether you love them or hate them, dandelions are among the most familiar plants in the world. They're one species that just about anyone can identify at a glance, as familiar to humans as the dog. Dandelions are, quite possibly, the most successful plants that exist, masters of survival worldwide. Before the invention of lawns, people praised the golden blossoms and lion-toothed leaves as a bounty of food, medicine and magic.

Gardeners often weeded out the grass to make room for the dandelions. But somewhere in the twentieth century, humans decided that the dandelion was a weed. Nowadays, they're also the most unpopular plant in the neighborhood – but it wasn't always that way. To show the benefits of the once-beloved plant, here are 10 ten things you might not know about dandelions.

1. Dandelions have deep roots in history throughout the ages. Ancient Egyptians, Greeks and Romans enjoyed the flower, and they have been used in Chinese traditional medicine for over a thousand years. Dandelions probably arrived in North America on the Mayflower – not as stowaways, but brought on purpose for their medicinal benefits.

2. Dandelions were world-famous for their beauty. They were a common and beloved garden flower in Europe, and the subject of many poems. In the terrifying New World, the cheerful face of the dandelion was a sweet reminder of home. In Japan for instance, whole horticultural societies formed to enjoy the beauty of dandelions and to develop exciting new varieties for gardeners.

3. Dandelions are a green and growing first aid kit. The use of dandelions in the healing arts goes so

far back that tracing its history is like trying to catch a dandelion seed as it floats over the grass. For millenniums, people have been using dandelion tonics to help body's liver remove toxins from the bloodstream. In olden times, dandelions were also prescribed for every ailment, from warts to the plague.

To this day, herbalists hail the dandelion as the perfect plant medicine: It is a gentle diuretic that provides nutrients and helps the digestive system function at peak efficiency.

4. Dandelions are more nutritious than most of the vegetables in your garden. They were named after lions because their lion-toothed leaves healed so many ailments, great and small: baldness, dandruff, toothache, sores, fevers, rotting gums, weakness, lethargy and depression. But it wasn't until the twentieth century was the underlying cause of many of these symptoms realized: vitamin deficiencies.

In eras when vitamin pills were unknown, vitamin deficiencies killed millions. In its time, "scurvy" was as dreaded a word as AIDS is today. Data from the U.S. Department of Agriculture reveal how dandelions probably helped alleviate many ailments: They have more vitamin A than spinach, more vitamin C than tomatoes, and are a powerhouse of iron, calcium and potassium.

5. Dandelions are good for your lawn. Their wide-spreading roots loosen hard-packed soil, aerate the earth and help reduce erosion. The deep taproot pulls nutrients such as calcium from deep in the soil and makes them available to other plants. While most think they're a lawn killer, dandelions actually fertilize the grass.

6. Dandelions are masters of survival. They can take root in places that seem little short of miraculous, and then are impossible to get rid of, as homeowners have found. But why is this plant so hard to kill? It's because they are fast growers.

The sunny yellow flowers go from bud to seed in days. Their lifespan is long, too — an individual plant can live for years, so the dandelion lurking in a corner of the playground might be older than the children running past it. The roots sink in deeper over the years, and can go down 15 feet.

Like the Hydra who sprouted two new heads for every one that was cut off, the roots clone when divided; a one-inch bit of dandelion root can grow a whole new dandelion. Dandelion leaves can shove their way though gravel and cement, and thrive in barren habitats.

7. Dandelions are among the most expensive items in the grocery store. Shops sell dried roots as a no-caffeine coffee substitute — for $31.75 a pound. Dandelions out-price prime rib, swordfish and lobster. They also appear in produce and other sections, and even at the liquor store. You can enjoy a complete meal, from salad greens to

dandelion quiche, followed by dandelion ice cream, washed down with dandelion wine.

If you over-indulge, a cup of dandelion tea is the perfect remedy, since dandelions help the liver flush hangover-inducing toxins from the body.

8. Herbicides used on lawns to kill dandelions take a terrible toll on wildlife. More than seven million wild birds are estimated to die annually due to the use of lawn pesticides. Lawns make up thirty million acres of the United States, and Americans use an estimated 80 million pounds of pesticides on them annually. The U.S. Fish and Wildlife Service reports that "homeowners use up to ten times more chemical pesticides per acre on their lawns than farmers use on crops."

9. But there's a safer way to have a dandelion-free lawn! Let the grass grow 3 or 4 inches tall to shade out the sun-loving dandelions, or use specialized tools like the Weed Hound to have a thriving, healthy yard that is safe for kids, pets and wildlife.

10. And at the end of the day, dandelions are just plain fun. The dandelion seems to be the flower earmarked for children: In a park or garden, it's the only flower a kid can pick without getting into trouble. A child in a field full of dandelions can practically never run out of things to do: Blowing on dandelion puffballs can tell you if it's time to go home, how many years until you get married, or how many children you'll have — and of course, if you catch a flying dandelion seed, you can make a wish.

DANDELION TEA: IS IT GOOD FOR YOU?

Dandelion is much more than just a weed growing in the yard. In fact, it has been cultivated for its culinary and medicinal benefits for centuries, and modern science has even begun corroborating some of the claims traditionally made about dandelion. Dandelion is very common in North America and most people can recognize it on sight. It's a hardy plant, growing easily in low-sunlight areas where others struggle.

The flowers, leaf, and root of dandelion can all be used to make dandelion tea. In parts of Europe and Asia, it's known as a folk remedy for:

- ✓ Urinary Tract Infections
- ✓ Inflammation
- ✓ Detoxing the Body
- ✓ The Common Cold

However, while modern science has lent some support to these and other traditional medicine claims about dandelion tea, much more research is needed.

Nutrition Information

One cup of raw dandelion contains:

- ✓ Calories: 25
- ✓ Protein: 1.5 grams
- ✓ Fat: 0.4 grams
- ✓ Carbohydrates: 5.1 grams
- ✓ Fiber: 1.9 grams
- ✓ Sugar: 0.4 grams
- ✓ Dandelion is a good source of:
- ✓ Beta-carotene
- ✓ Magnesium
- ✓ Calcium
- ✓ Iron
- ✓ Zinc

Dandelion is also an excellent source of Vitamin A. Studies have shown that Vitamin A may lower the risk of conditions like cataracts, diarrhea, measles, and breast cancer.

Potential Health Benefits of Dandelion Tea

Dandelion is a rich source of vitamins and minerals. However, the same thing that makes dandelion so potent can also create complications for people with certain medical conditions. Research has found a number of potential health benefits to drinking dandelion tea:

Anti-inflammatory Effects

Dandelion contains taraxasterol, a compound known for having significant antioxidant properties that combat inflammation. Taraxasterol can help regulate your white blood cells and keep them from triggering inflammation unnecessarily.

Lower Blood Pressure

Dandelion tea is an excellent source of potassium, a mineral and electrolyte that stimulates the heartbeat. Potassium may help the kidney filter toxins more effectively and improve blood flow.

Improved Liver Health

The polysaccharides in dandelion are known to reduce stress on the liver and support its ability to produce bile. They also help your liver filter potentially harmful chemicals out of your food.

Immune System Support

Dandelion is also a good source of Vitamin C, one of the most helpful vitamins for the immune system. The presence of Vitamin C may account for its reported effectiveness against seasonal colds.

Potential Risks of Dandelion Tea

Because dandelion tea has such potent ingredients, you should consult with your doctor before taking it or any other supplement. Consider the following before preparing or drinking dandelion tea:

Daisy Allergies

If you're allergic to other plants in the daisy family — like daisies, marigolds, or chrysanthemums — you will also be allergic to dandelion.

Pregnancy Concerns

The effects of dandelion tea on someone who is pregnant or breast-feeding are inconclusive. If you're pregnant or breastfeeding a baby, it is best to look for an alternative.

Medication Interference

Avoid dandelion tea if you're already taking a diuretic as their actions may be compounded. Since dandelion has natural diuretic properties, it may interfere with the action of lithium and similar medications. Dandelion tea should also be avoided if you're taking antibiotics like Cipro, Levaquin, Noroxin, and others.

Liver and Kidney Function

If you're being treated for liver or kidney issues, you should avoid consuming dandelion or dandelion tea except with their doctor's permission. Dandelion could increase the risk of complications for someone who has kidney disease, in particular.

Blood Pressure and Clotting

Because the potassium in dandelion may impact blood flow and clotting, it's best to avoid dandelion tea if you're taking blood-thinner medication. For the same reason, someone who is taking blood pressure medication should avoid dandelion tea.

DANDELION LEAF EXTRACT EVERYTHING YOU NEED TO KNOW

You will have certainly seen dandelion leafs before as they really look striking when in the field. But did you know they have many health benefits too? This is why you're seeing dandelion leaf extract appearing in many health products as they could provide a simple addition to your health and wellness routine. In this guide book, however, we will be narrowing our focus on dandelion leaves, their benefits and why it's one of core ingredients in some tonic.

Understanding Dandelion Leaf Extract

Taken from the leaves of the dandelion plant, the dandelion leaf extract is often used in dietary supplements as a diuretic for digestive problems.

These yellow florets are also known as Taraxacum spp. and Taraxacum officinale is the most common species of dandelions. Although dandelions have gained a bad reputation for being a pesky garden weed, these white puffballs are surprisingly beneficial to your health.

Renowned and widely used in traditional herbal medicine, dandelions have long been used to treat liver, gallbladder and bile problems.

Benefits of Dandelion Leaves

Don't let these tiny golden flowers fool you, they are not just stubborn garden weeds. People have used dandelions for centuries, administered as a natural remedy used in tea, juice or tonic. Recently, its multitude of health benefits has become more well-known and it is now being added in various health supplements such as supergreen powders.

Highly Nutritious

Dandelion leaf extract are full of Vitamin A, an essential nutrient in regards to maintaining your eye health. Dandelions contain a red-orange pigment, also known as beta-carotene, which is converted into Vitamin A in our bodies. Vitamin A promotes healthier skin, boosts our immune systems and most significantly, aids in eye health and vision.

According to a study in the Journal of the American Medical Association, 5,836 older adults showed a link between a higher intake of Vitamin A and a significantly lower risk of macular degeneration caused by aging. A rich source of vitamins and minerals, this includes Vitamin C, Vitamin K, Vitamin E, potassium, iron, calcium, magnesium, zinc and phosphorus. Dandelion leaves can be useful in boosting your intake of minerals.

Although packed full of nutritious goodness, one of the most nutrient dense ingredients is still

Spirulina. We check out this powerhouse greens and protein nutrient in our benefits of Spirulina article.

Antioxidants

As mentioned previously, dandelions are full of beta-carotene. Beta-carotene is in fact, also a form of carotenoids that act as antioxidants. Antioxidants are important as they neutralize or protect you from the effects of free radicals in your body. Free radicals are toxic by-products of metabolism that can cause "oxidative stress", leading to cell damage. Thus, the body requires antioxidants to counter the negative effects of free radicals.

Dandelions are also high in polyphenols, another type of antioxidant. The flowers contain the highest concentration of polyphenols, but it can also be found in the leaves of the dandelion.

Decreases Water Weight

Dandelion greens are a natural diuretic; they increase urination, reducing bloating and levels of water retention in the body. According to a study conducted by the Department of Herbal Medicine at the Tai Sophia Institute of Maryland (1), consuming dandelion extract has been shown to significantly increase the frequency of urination for up to 5 hours. It's diuretic properties can help the liver to flush toxins out of the body and also reduce the risk of urinary tract infections.

However, the study was conducted with only 17 participants, over a short period of time. More research has to be done to prove its effectiveness.

Aid in Weight Loss

Consuming dandelion greens can inhibit fat absorption in the body, by disrupting enzyme activity. According to a study in the Nutrition Research and Practice (2), dandelion leaves showed strong inhibitory behavior towards pancreatic lipase, the digestive enzyme that breaks down fat molecules in the body. Results showed that the dandelion extract had a drastic effect on the pancreatic lipase activity, reducing it by a whopping 86%, excreting larger amounts of fats.

Furthermore, lipase is also the digestive enzyme that breaks down triglycerides into fatty acids. The fall in lipase activity due to dandelion leaves can lead to increased excretion of triglycerides, hence, reduce the risk of heart disease.

Promotes a Healthy Liver

Studies on animals have found that dandelions are able to protect the liver from damage in the presence of toxic substances and stress. In a 2010 study (3), when mice were exposed to dangerous levels of acetaminophen, also known as Tylenol, the dandelion leaf extract prevented and protected the liver from oxidative damage and inflammation.

May Boost your Immune System

Although research has not been conducted extensively, some studies have shown links that dandelion extract has reduced the ability of viruses to reproduce and replicate. The antimicrobial and antiviral properties of dandelions could be able to protect the body against bacteria and fight against infections. More in-depth research has to be done in order to draw more definite conclusions about the medicinal properties of the dandelion.

Side-effects of Dandelion Leaves

Some people can have an allergic reaction to dandelion if it is consumed or applied to the skin. If you are sensitive to flowers from the same family such as ragweed, daisies, chrysanthemums or marigolds, it's safer for your health to not consume dandelion leaves. When consumed or applied, please discontinue immediately if symptoms such as redness of the skin, itching, or swelling occur.

Bring the suspected product and talk to your healthcare provider as soon as possible. Dandelion leaves might also interact with other medications, such as certain diuretics and antibiotics. If you're on any prescribed drugs, speak to your healthcare provider before consuming and dandelion-related products. Do note that the exact amount safe to consume is still not certain. Research is still lacking in this area.

The effectiveness and strength vary according to each product, hence it is always best to follow the recommended doses written on the bottle. Speak to your nutritionist if you have any concerns.

Where Can I Buy Some?

You can find dandelion leaves in a salad bowl at times, but it is not widely available. It is definitely not the safest to simply pick the plant from your garden either, due to the potential use of pesticides, or the presence of animal excretion. But the Food and Drug Administration (FDA) has stated that dandelions are generally safe to use in food products.

Due to its array of health benefits, the dandelion leaf extract is included in various health supplements, often found in Supergreen powders.

EASY DANDELION RECIPES

FROM TEA TO PESTO

Between the vitamins, folate, calcium, and potassium, these dandelion recipes are as nutritious as they are delicious. So if you've never cooked with this little weed before, now's the time to give it a try! Surprisingly, dandelions are a powerful superfood packed with vitamins, minerals, fiber, and antioxidants. Best of all, they're a super versatile ingredient. And you can use it all, from the petals to the roots.

I'm talking everything from savory main dishes and hearty soups to drinks and even sweet treats. So, why not whip up one of these magical dandelion recipes instead of just mowing them away?

1. Sautéed Dandelion Greens Roman Style (Cicoria Alla Romana)

Dandelion greens are a staple in Roman cuisine. They're cheap yet packed with excellent health benefits and rich flavor. And with just a handful of ingredients, this recipe transforms these garden greens into something magical. Spicy, peppery, and a bit bitter, sautéed dandelion greens pair perfectly with almost any dish.

2. Dandelion Honey From Flowers

Did you know you can make vegan honey with dandelions, sugar, vanilla, and a bit of lemon? The taste is delicate and unique, with floral and citrus notes. It's a pale golden color and has a delightful, earthy flavor. Use it in tea or your favorite baked goods.

3. Vegan Dandelion Bread

Meet the perfect vegan bread recipe for anyone missing their daily fix of carbs. Dandelion flower petals add light, citrusy flavors to an otherwise sweet treat. Plus, it has subtle bitterness that'll delight your taste buds until the last bite. The best part is that it's not too dense, unlike some other vegan bread recipes.

4. Infused Dandelion Vinegar

It's time to start infusing your life – and your dinners – with dandelion vinegar! And all you need to do is infuse white wine vinegar with fresh dandelion flowers. It mellows the acidity, making it mildly sweet and slightly bitter. This unique vinegar is the perfect addition to salads for a bright touch of springtime.

5. Dandelion Jelly

Looking for a fresh, new jelly recipe you can easily make at home? Then, dandelion jelly is the thing. These bright yellow flowers make this jelly taste a little like honey, with a brilliant lemony kick. It's a soft, spreadable jam that tastes like spring in every bite! Best of all, this recipe uses minimal ingredients that are probably in your pantry already!

6. Dandelion Tea

Delight your senses with a cup of dandelion tea! It's a delicious blend of dandelion petals steeped in boiling water. Sweeten it with sugar or dandelion honey for even more of that floral goodness. This refreshing beverage is perfect for any time of the day. Serve it hot or cold and sip to your heart's content.

7. Dandelion Cupcakes with Lemon Buttercream Frosting

These cupcakes are the perfect marriage of sweet and sour. The frosting is creamy and tart, while the cupcakes have a hint of floral sweetness. They're moist, fluffy, and come out of the oven with a perfect golden brown goodness. These little beauties are ideal for a picnic or Easter brunch.

8. Dandelion Pesto

Dandelion pesto is the perfect way to add a little herby zing to your next meal. It's nutrient-rich, full of flavor, and packed with bright green goodness. This recipe features dandelion greens and traditional pesto ingredients. However, cloves and turmeric powder are also in the mix, making it earthy and warm. Toss it in your favorite pasta, spread it on bread, or try it with chicken or fish; you can't go wrong with this recipe.

9. Sautéed Dandelion Greens with Eggs

Start your day right and throw some dandelion greens in with your morning eggs. This recipe is my favorite way to welcome spring, and it's loaded with goodness. Between the rich flavor, bitter notes, and protein from the eggs, it's light and refreshing but still super satisfying! I especially love the creamy and salty feta on top!

10. Hanger Steak with Dandelion, Arugula, and Grana Padano

Looking for an elegant date night meal to impress your honey? This hanger steak recipe is just the ticket. The bitter, slightly sweet greens pair wonderfully with the rich, meaty steak. It's definitely for anyone who likes spinach or asparagus with their steak dinner. You'll also add arugula and Grana Padano cheese for an extra boost of bitter and umami goodness.

11. Roasted Dandelion Root Coffee with Fennel and Cinnamon

Have you been looking for something fun to replace your morning cup of joe? Then you're in luck! Dandelion is technically a weed, but I think it's a pretty amazing one. Not only is it pretty, but its roots are full of vitamins and minerals, making it an excellent coffee alternative! The root is roasted and paired with fennel and cinnamon. Each sip will surely wake up your senses with its unique flavor!

12. Dandelion Mocha

Craving the taste of coffee but hate that jittery feeling you get from caffeine? Then, a cup of dandelion mocha is just what you need. It'll warm you up on a chilly day and give you an energy boost. Serve it with a slice of honey bun cake for the perfect mid-morning pick-me-up.

13. Dandelion Mead Recipe (Dandelion Wine Made With Honey)

This recipe is for you if you've ever wanted to try homemade mead. It's easy to make and even easier to drink. Featuring honey, dandelion petals, lemon, and champagne yeast, it's sweet and citrusy with floral notes, making it the perfect summer drink.

14. Dandelion Soda

Dandelion soda is a naturally fermented drink with a ginger bug starter (a starter culture similar to sourdough), so it's got some kick. This carbonated tonic is made with dandelion petals, sugar, and lemon. It's perfect if you like a little fizz in your drink but want something unique. A cold glass of this dandelion soda will surely bring a burst of freshness in every sip.

15. Dandelion Wine

Dandelion wine is a light, refreshing beverage perfect for summer picnics and beach days. It's made with fresh dandelion flowers, which are known for their natural detoxifying properties. They're distilled into a sweet, golden liquid that's bright and citrusy. Sip and swirl this rich dandelion wine for a unique, hearty experience!

16. Cumin-Scented Lentils With Sausage and Dandelion Green

These cumin-scented lentils are a terrific way to mix up your dinner routine. It's full of fiber and protein, and it's super filling to boot. The dandelion greens add an earthy flavor and the sausage bring smoky meatiness. It's guaranteed to warm you up on a chilly day.

17. Dandelion Greens + Bean Skillet

Packed with greens, herbs, spices, and aromatics, these greens and beans combine savory and earthy flavors to tickle your tastebuds. Made in one skillet, this is a terrific vegan meal. That said, it's fabulous with some roasted chicken or fish.

18. Dandelion Root Muffins

These muffins are hearty, bold, and not overly sweet. I think they're perfect for breakfast with a bit of almond butter on top! Made with dandelion root, each muffin is packed with natural ingredients that are filling and nutritious. Plus, they're fluffy, paleo-friendly, and gluten-free! Serve them with a cup of tea for a hearty breakfast or afternoon snack.

19. Dandelion Shortbread Cookies

Dandelion shortbread cookies are a treat for the eyes and the palate. These delicate melt-in-your-mouth treats are sure to become one of your favorites. The buttery cookie base is loaded with dandelion petals, giving the dough a delicate, slightly nutty flavor and a pop of color. Each bite of these cookies brings sunshine and sweetness to brighten your day.

20. Dandelion Fritters

These fritters are so good; you'll want to eat them for every meal! They're super unique and fun, with a soft flavor from the dandelion flowers and plenty of herbs and spices. The fluffy texture of the batter and the crispy outer coating make these fritters irresistible.

21. Creamy Dandelion Soup {Paleo, Vegan, Whole30}

When you're in the mood for a light and creamy soup, this dandelion soup fits the bill. The combination of dandelion greens and cashews makes it super creamy while still healthy. It's also loaded with cauliflower and celery for a nutrient-rich dish. With just a few simple ingredients, you'll have a delicious meal to warm your soul in no time.

22. Dandelion Egg Noodles

These dandelion egg noodles are a delicious, easy-to-make treat for spring! And all you need is eggs, dandelion greens, and flour. They're richer and more flavorful than traditional egg noodles, with a bright green color to boot. Serve them with any pasta sauce, and they're sure to please.

23. Pici Pasta with Dandelion Greens

Looking for an extra-filling pasta dish that's a breeze to make? I've got you covered! A bowl of this pasta is so simple, yet it's amazingly rich. You'll sauté dandelion greens with garlic and olive oil until they're tender. Then toss them with pici pasta and finish with cheese and bread crumbs. Yum!

24. Pickled Dandelion Capers

Dandelion capers are briny, salty, and great on salads or as a garnish for other dishes. This recipe uses dandelion buds that are fermented for 7 to 10 days. The result is a flavorful caper that you can store in the fridge for months!

25. Dandelion Green Smoothie

This dandelion green smoothie is sure to wake you up! It's bright, sweet, and refreshing, making it the perfect way to start the day. Loaded with frozen berries, bananas, and dandelion greens, it also features a dash of cinnamon for extra richness. Every sip of this smoothie will give you a boost of energy to get through your day. Feel free to add a dash of dandelion honey if you want it sweeter!

26. Dandelion Cupcakes with Sunflower Seeds

Dandelion cupcakes with sunflower seeds are the perfect treat for a sunny day! These soft, sweet, and moist cupcakes fill your mouth with dandelion flavor, while the sunflower seeds are a delightfully crunchy contrast to the fluffy cake. Between the vibrant golden brown color and fresh edible flowers, these cupcakes are a real treat.

27. Dandelion Green Pesto, Fresh Fig, and Gorgonzola Pizza with Prosciutto

Sweet figs, sharp, biting gorgonzola, and earthy dandelion pesto with gooey fontina cheese and salty prosciutto? Yeah, it's as scrumptious as it sounds. This unique pizza is topped with fresh flowers for a pop of color and hearty floral notes. One bite, and you'll crave it again and again.

28. Greens-Stuffed, Cheese-Stuffed Quesadilla

Stuffed with a delicious blend of greens and cheese, this quesadilla is my favorite way to get my daily dose of veggies. I enjoy the flavor of corn tortillas, but you can use any you like best. Either way, it'll burst with flavor and melty cheese.

29. Healthy Potato Salad with Dandelion Greens

Forget the usual fatty potato salad and try this green twist for your next BBQ. This potato salad is loaded with dandelion greens, garlic, ginger, coriander, turmeric, cumin, and smoked paprika. So it's bright, spiced, and bursting with fragrant deliciousness. I think this is best served warm with the potatoes nice and crispy.

30. Dandelion Greens Sauté with Bacon & Raisins

Dandelion greens are a nutritious addition to your diet, but like kale, they can be bitter and tough. Luckily, this recipe will help you prepare them! From the spices and raisins to the smoky bacon, it's ideal for parties and BBQs. Pair it with grilled meat or seafood for a hearty meal.

Best Ways to Cook with Dandelions (+ Recipe Collection)

Between the vitamins, folate, calcium, and potassium, these bright and easy dandelion recipes are as nutritious as they are delicious.

Recipes:

- ✓ Sautéed Dandelion Greens Roman Style (Cicoria Alla Romana)
- ✓ Dandelion Honey From Flowers
- ✓ Vegan Dandelion Bread
- ✓ Infused Dandelion Vinegar
- ✓ Dandelion Jelly
- ✓ Dandelion Tea
- ✓ Dandelion Cupcakes with Lemon Buttercream Frosting
- ✓ Dandelion Pesto
- ✓ Sautéed Dandelion Greens with Eggs
- ✓ Hanger Steak with Dandelion, Arugula, and Grana Padano

- ✓ Roasted Dandelion Root Coffee with Fennel and Cinnamon
- ✓ Dandelion Mocha
- ✓ Dandelion Mead Recipe (Dandelion Wine Made With Honey)
- ✓ Dandelion Soda
- ✓ Dandelion Wine
- ✓ Cumin-Scented Lentils With Sausage and Dandelion Green
- ✓ Dandelion Greens + Bean Skillet
- ✓ Dandelion Root Muffins
- ✓ Dandelion Shortbread Cookies
- ✓ Dandelion Fritters
- ✓ Creamy Dandelion Soup {Paleo, Vegan, Whole30}
- ✓ Dandelion Egg Noodles
- ✓ Pici Pasta with Dandelion Greens
- ✓ Pickled Dandelion Capers
- ✓ Dandelion Green Smoothie
- ✓ Dandelion Cupcakes with Sunflower Seeds

- ✓ Dandelion Green Pesto, Fresh Fig, and Gorgonzola Pizza with Prosciutto
- ✓ Greens-Stuffed, Cheese-Stuffed Quesadilla
- ✓ Healthy Potato Salad with Dandelion Greens
- ✓ Dandelion Greens Sauté with Bacon & Raisins

Instructions:

- ✓ Select your favorite recipe.
- ✓ Organize all the required ingredients.
- ✓ Prep a delicious dandelion recipe in 30 minutes or less!

CONCLUSION

Dandelion, also known as Taraxacum officinale, is a type of plant that belongs to the daisy family. Despite being considered little more than a weed by many, dandelion packs in some impressive health benefits when it comes to supporting the digestive and immune systems. What can dandelion treat? While it's not treated as a drug, as a supplement it offers protection against oxidative stress, liver disease, high cholesterol and blood pressure, high blood sugar, cancer, kidney issues, and infections.

Dandelion root can be taken in pill or extract supplement form or used to brew a hot cup of caffeine-free coffee or tea. Dandelions require sun and disturbed soil to thrive. That's why they seem to "look for" human activities: roadsides, construction sites, parking lots – and lawns. Having escaped the herb gardens a few decades ago, they now seem to be on a quest to get back into the yards they once abandoned.

Dandelions probably will never be eradicated, but we can learn to be more at ease with dandelions and other wild things – and maybe even to love them a little.